Meta's Orion AR Glasses

From Virtual Assistants to Immersive Holograms: The Next Leap in Augmented Reality

Roger A. Shawn

Copyright

Copyright © Roger A. Shawn. All rights reserved.

No part of this publication may be reproduced, distributed, or transmitted in any form or by any means, including photocopying, recording, or other electronic or mechanical methods, without the prior written permission of the publisher, except in the case of brief quotations embodied in critical reviews and certain other non-commercial uses permitted by copyright law.

Table of Content

Copyright.. 2
Table of Content...3
Introduction.. 5
Chapter One...8
The Genesis of Orion – Meta's Visionary Project... 8
Chapter Two.. 11
Unpacking the Hardware – Glasses, Compute Puck, and Neural Interfaces........ 11
Chapter Three..15
Technologies Pioneered by Meta for Orion 15
Chapter Four.. 18
The AR Experience –................................. 18
A Day in the Life with Orion...................... 18
Chapter Five...22
The Future of Human Interaction and AR. 22
Chapter Six.. 26
Challenges and Limitations of Orion......... 26

Chapter Seven..30
The Path Ahead – Consumer Adoption and Future Versions..30
Chapter Eight...34
Meta's Vision for the AR Landscape..........34
Conclusion..37

Introduction

Stepping into the Meta Connect Conference, the atmosphere buzzed with a sense of anticipation. The air felt electric, with the world's top innovators and tech enthusiasts gathered in one place, waiting for the reveal that promised to reshape the future. All eyes were drawn to the main stage, where the spotlight would soon fall on something that could transform the way we interact with the digital world. When the Orion AR glasses were unveiled, it wasn't just a product launch—it was a declaration of how far technology had come. These glasses stood as a symbol of what's possible when vision meets determination, with years of research and countless dollars funneled into creating something that seemed straight out of science fiction.

The Orion AR glasses, sleek and deceptively simple, are anything but ordinary. Behind their minimalist design lies an extraordinary blend of cutting-edge technologies that have never been brought together before in such a compact form. Meta has packed years of innovation into a lightweight, wearable device that promises to push the boundaries of personal technology. These glasses, weighing just 98 grams, carry a price tag of $10,000 per prototype, highlighting the sophistication of the hardware. With the ability to project holograms into your field of vision and respond to neural inputs with near-instant precision, the Orion AR glasses represent a leap forward that once seemed impossible.

This book dives deep into what makes these glasses so revolutionary, but more importantly, why this matters for everyone, not just the tech enthusiasts. We're standing on the brink of a new technological age, where augmented reality isn't just an abstract idea—it's about to become part of our daily lives. From replacing smartphones to transforming the way we work, communicate, and even play, the Orion AR glasses mark the beginning of a future that's closer than you think. Understanding the power of this technology is crucial for anyone who wants to be ahead of the curve, because these glasses aren't just another piece of tech—they're the future. Keep reading, and you'll see why.

Chapter One

The Genesis of Orion – Meta's Visionary Project

Meta's initial vision for the Orion AR glasses was nothing short of audacious. The goal wasn't merely to enhance existing technology but to create something so transformative it could replace the smartphone itself. Meta imagined a future where personal computing wouldn't be confined to a handheld device. Instead, the power to communicate, work, and interact with the digital world would be seamlessly integrated into something as simple as a pair of glasses. This idea wasn't about incremental change—it was about redefining the relationship between humans and technology, making digital interactions as natural as the air we breathe.

From the very beginning, Meta knew the road to this kind of breakthrough would be filled with challenges. The sheer scope of the project meant venturing into uncharted technological territory. They set out with the understanding that success wasn't guaranteed. In fact, the odds were stacked heavily against them. The team gave themselves only a slim 10% chance of achieving their ambitious goal. Still, they pressed forward, driven by the possibility of creating something that could truly change the world. What followed was an incredible journey of technological breakthroughs. Over the course of development, they pioneered ten entirely new technologies, each one a crucial piece of the puzzle. From the creation of advanced microLED displays to developing neural interfaces that could detect and respond to the user's intent, every step brought them closer to the vision of a fully immersive AR experience.

Orion wasn't just a product—it became a symbol of the future. Those involved in its creation began to refer to it as a "time machine," and not without reason. The technology embedded in these glasses was so far ahead of its time that it provided a glimpse of what personal computing could become years down the line. The high cost of development, with each prototype costing around $10,000, emphasized the advanced nature of the project. It was clear that Orion was more than just a technological leap; it was a portal to the future. The term "time machine" encapsulated the awe and wonder that came with seeing what could one day be a common part of daily life. Each time someone put on the glasses, they were stepping into a world that many thought was still decades away.

Chapter Two

Unpacking the Hardware – Glasses, Compute Puck, and Neural Interfaces

At the heart of Meta's Orion AR glasses lies an intricate system designed to seamlessly blend digital content with the physical world. The glasses themselves may appear sleek and lightweight, but their inner workings are a marvel of advanced engineering. Central to their functionality are optical systems, micro projectors, and waveguides that work together to project vivid holograms into the user's field of vision. These holograms are not just floating images; they are anchored in the environment around you, making it feel as though digital objects are part of the physical space. The micro projectors use cutting-edge technology to ensure high brightness and color accuracy, essential for creating clear and lifelike images, even in various lighting conditions. The waveguides, made from silicon carbide, act as the medium through which these images are delivered, allowing the user to experience a wide field of view without distortion. Every glance feels natural, as the system tracks eye movements and adjusts the holograms accordingly, creating an immersive experience that redefines how we interact with digital content.

Supporting the glasses is the compute puck, a compact and wireless device that serves as the brain of the system. While the glasses handle the display, the compute puck is responsible for running the applications and managing data. This device allows the glasses to remain lightweight and comfortable by offloading the heavy computational work. It communicates with the glasses through a custom-designed wireless protocol, ensuring low-latency data transfer, which is crucial for maintaining the fluidity of the AR experience. Users can keep the puck in a bag or pocket, allowing them to move freely without being tethered to any bulky hardware. The compute puck not only powers the visual aspect of the glasses but also supports a wide range of interactions, making the experience feel seamless and responsive.

One of the most innovative elements of the Orion system is the neural wristband, a groundbreaking piece of technology that adds a whole new dimension to user interaction. The wristbands utilize electromyography (EMG) to detect electrical signals sent from the brain to the muscles, allowing users to control the glasses through subtle gestures. This means that even with your hands in your pockets or by your side, you can still interact with the digital environment simply by moving your fingers or making slight wrist movements. The wristbands are designed to be comfortable and discreet, enabling intuitive control without the need for traditional input devices like controllers or keyboards. The precision of the EMG system allows for a range of actions, from scrolling through menus to selecting objects, all without breaking the natural flow of the AR experience. This hands-free control is a significant step forward in making augmented reality a practical and immersive tool for everyday use.

Chapter Three

Technologies Pioneered by Meta for Orion

Meta's development of the Orion AR glasses required pioneering technologies that pushed the boundaries of what was previously thought possible. One of the key innovations was the invention of microLED displays. These displays were designed to deliver exceptionally high brightness levels and remarkable color accuracy, both essential for creating lifelike holograms. Unlike traditional LED screens, which tend to struggle in bright environments, Meta's microLEDs maintain clarity and vibrancy even in direct sunlight. This was critical for augmented reality, where the projected images must compete with the natural light around the user. Each microLED was meticulously engineered to be both powerful and energy-efficient, ensuring that the holograms appeared sharp and vivid without draining excessive power.

In tandem with the microLEDs, Meta introduced silicon carbide waveguides as a key component of Orion's optical system. Silicon carbide is not typically associated with optics, but its unique properties made it an ideal choice for this groundbreaking application. Its high refractive index allowed for the creation of a wide field of view, which was crucial for providing an immersive AR experience. Additionally, silicon carbide is lightweight and incredibly durable, ensuring that the waveguides could withstand everyday wear and tear while delivering crystal-clear visuals. The material's ability to minimize the loss of light within the waveguide also helped reduce visual artifacts like ghosting and rainbow effects, which are common challenges in augmented reality displays. The result was a level of clarity and optical performance that set a new standard for AR technology.

To power such advanced features while keeping the device lightweight and efficient, Meta developed custom silicon chips specifically for Orion. These chips were designed to manage power efficiency, allowing the glasses to run on minimal battery power without sacrificing performance. In augmented reality, where continuous data processing and high-resolution imaging are essential, power consumption becomes a major concern. Meta's custom silicon chips addressed this issue by significantly reducing the energy needed to operate the glasses. These chips handled everything from managing the microLED displays to processing the data coming from the sensors, all while maintaining a low thermal footprint. This innovation not only extended the battery life of the glasses but also made them more comfortable to wear, as the components generated less heat, further enhancing the overall user experience.

Chapter Four

The AR Experience –

A Day in the Life with Orion

Imagine putting on the Orion AR glasses and immediately stepping into a world where the digital blends seamlessly with reality. You glance around and notice a virtual chessboard floating on the coffee table in front of you, waiting for you to make the next move. The pieces are as solid and tangible as the table itself, but you know they are merely holograms. Across the room, a friend appears in a video call, their image anchored in place as though they are physically present, yet they could be miles away. Without disrupting your surroundings, a to-do list hovers just within your line of sight, subtly reminding you of tasks for the day, or perhaps an email notification appears, allowing you to skim through it without missing a beat. This is the immersive experience that Orion promises, where holograms don't feel like intrusions but natural extensions of your environment.

The true power of the Orion glasses, however, lies in how seamlessly artificial intelligence integrates with augmented reality. With AI constantly processing the world around you, it's as if your environment is alive with information. Need to know where you left your keys? Orion can query your environment, recalling the last place you set them down. Virtual assistants within the glasses can anticipate your needs before you even ask, whether it's suggesting a nearby café when you're out for a walk or reminding you of upcoming appointments. The AI operates quietly in the background, feeding you the information you need when you need it, without ever pulling you out of the moment. The glasses can read the context of your day, learning your preferences and offering solutions tailored to your habits and routines.

Orion's capabilities extend far beyond just flashy holograms. Picture walking into a business meeting where the presentation notes appear in your peripheral vision, or perhaps the entire presentation is projected on the conference room table, fully interactive and accessible to everyone wearing Orion. There's no need to pull out a phone or laptop; everything you need is right there in your view. Later, while grocery shopping, the glasses scan the shelves, providing real-time price comparisons or nutritional information. You can compile a virtual shopping list that appears as you move through the aisles, making mundane tasks more efficient. The potential for Orion to replace the smartphone becomes evident when you realize that everything you typically rely on your phone for—communication, navigation, scheduling, and entertainment—can be accessed with a simple glance or subtle gesture, all while keeping your hands free and your attention focused on the world around you.

In essence, a day with Orion is a day where the boundaries between the digital and physical worlds dissolve, where every interaction feels more intuitive and less obstructive. From handling work tasks with greater efficiency to navigating daily life with personalized AI assistance, the Orion AR glasses offer a glimpse into a future where technology adapts seamlessly to our needs, creating an experience that is as immersive as it is practical.

Chapter Five

The Future of Human Interaction and AR

Meta envisions a future where the smartphone, once considered the pinnacle of personal technology, becomes obsolete, replaced by something far more immersive and integrated into daily life: the Orion AR glasses. The concept is revolutionary—a device that doesn't require you to reach into your pocket or stare down at a screen, but instead allows you to interact with the digital world while remaining fully present in your physical surroundings. By seamlessly blending augmented reality into the environment around you, Orion offers a more contextual experience than any smartphone ever could. Whether it's checking notifications, making video calls, or navigating through a city, Orion allows you to do it all without disrupting your connection to the world. This shift towards AR represents Meta's belief that personal technology should enhance reality, not distract from it.

The rapid rise of artificial intelligence has been a game-changer for augmented reality, transforming it into something more versatile and deeply integrated into how we live. With Orion, AI works quietly in the background, constantly learning and adapting to your habits, routines, and environment. It's this synergy between AI and AR that makes Orion truly revolutionary. For instance, while you go about your day, the AI can anticipate your needs before you even have to ask—reminding you of an appointment as you pass by the building or helping you find a misplaced item by scanning the room for clues. This combination of AI and AR allows for an intuitive experience that blends the best of both technologies, offering real-time, relevant information that's accessible with a simple glance. The possibilities are endless, from augmented learning to smart cities that interact with you through your AR glasses, making everyday life smarter and more efficient.

Orion doesn't just have the potential to replace smartphones, it could completely transform the way we communicate and interact with one another. In a world where these glasses become commonplace, virtual meetings would feel far more personal and interactive. Instead of staring at a screen, you could engage in a video call where the person appears in your room, as though they're sitting right in front of you. Shared AR experiences could take social gatherings to a whole new level—imagine playing a board game where the pieces come to life, or watching a movie with friends where the screen is projected in mid-air, visible to everyone. Even in professional settings, the glasses could facilitate richer collaboration, allowing coworkers to share virtual models and designs in real-time, regardless of their location.

The social impact of such technology could be profound. No longer would people be glued to their phones, disconnected from those around them. Instead, AR could encourage more face-to-face interactions, allowing digital content to complement rather than replace human connection. Whether enhancing remote communication or enriching in-person experiences, Orion could fundamentally change how we relate to one another in a digitally saturated world, bridging the gap between the virtual and physical in ways we're only beginning to imagine.

Chapter Six

Challenges and Limitations of Orion

While the Orion AR glasses represent a groundbreaking leap in technology, they come with their own set of challenges and limitations that could delay widespread consumer adoption. One of the most significant barriers is the cost of production. Each Orion prototype currently costs around $10,000 to make, a price point that makes it far from practical for the average consumer. This staggering price is largely driven by the advanced technologies packed into each pair of glasses, from custom silicon chips to microLED displays and silicon carbide waveguides. These components are cutting-edge and expensive to produce, especially at such a small scale. While Meta's long-term goal is to reduce these costs and bring Orion to a broader market, it's clear that the high price tag will limit adoption in the immediate future. Only with further development and larger-scale production can these glasses become more affordable and accessible to the masses.

Another significant hurdle is battery life. Currently, the Orion glasses can only run for about two hours on a single charge, which limits their usability throughout the day. For a device intended to replace smartphones, this short battery life is a critical issue that Meta will need to address. The challenge is finding a balance between power and form factor. Packing more battery life into the glasses without making them bulkier or uncomfortable to wear is no easy task. Meta is already working on improvements, but for Orion to become a viable option for everyday use, the battery will need to last much longer, and the overall design must be lightweight enough to wear for extended periods without causing fatigue.

In addition to cost and battery life, there are still technical limitations in the display system that need refinement. One issue that early users have reported is ghosting—an optical artifact where remnants of previous images linger on the display, creating a blurred or double-vision effect. This can disrupt the immersive experience and make certain interactions feel less fluid. Additionally, the current resolution of the microLED displays, while impressive, doesn't yet match the sharpness people expect from modern screens. Text, for instance, can appear less crisp, and fine details may be difficult to discern. While Meta is already working on addressing these issues, such as improving the display resolution and minimizing visual artifacts, these imperfections underscore the fact that Orion is still very much a work in progress.

These challenges, from the high production cost to technical limitations, illustrate that while Orion is an incredible technological achievement, there's still a long road ahead before it can reach its full potential as a consumer product. Meta's engineers are undoubtedly aware of these hurdles and are actively working on solutions, but the path from prototype to mainstream adoption will require both time and further innovation.

Chapter Seven

The Path Ahead – Consumer Adoption and Future Versions

Looking ahead, Meta's vision for the future of Orion involves refining the technology to make it more accessible for the mass market. The current version of Orion, while impressive, is a prototype with a hefty price tag and a design that's not quite suited for everyday wear. Meta's engineers are already hard at work on the next version, which aims to be thinner, lighter, and more affordable. The goal is to create a pair of AR glasses that are sleek enough to wear all day without discomfort and powerful enough to handle the demands of modern personal computing. Achieving this balance is key to unlocking the potential for mass-market adoption, as the current model, while revolutionary, is still a glimpse of what the future could hold.

One of the most significant shifts will likely be in pricing. For Orion to become a household name, the cost will need to come down from the current $10,000 per prototype to something more in line with high-end consumer electronics. Speculation suggests that Meta could aim to price future versions of Orion in the range of high-end smartphones or laptops, potentially between $1,500 and $2,000. This would position Orion as a premium product, accessible to tech enthusiasts and early adopters, while still being within reach of consumers who are willing to invest in the next big leap in personal technology. Meta's strategy will likely involve a gradual rollout, starting with a high-end model that paves the way for more affordable versions as production scales and the technology becomes less expensive to manufacture.

In addition to refining Orion itself, Meta is also likely to transfer some of the breakthrough technologies developed for these AR glasses into other products within their lineup. The advancements in microLED displays, custom silicon, and AI integration could easily find their way into more affordable devices like Meta's Ray-Ban Stories or the Quest headsets. These products already serve as stepping stones for AR and VR technology, and incorporating Orion's innovations would enhance their capabilities while making AR more accessible to a broader audience. This technology transfer could allow Meta to reach consumers at various price points, ensuring that while Orion remains a premium device, its core innovations can benefit a wider range of users. By trickling down these technologies, Meta can drive the evolution of augmented and virtual reality across multiple platforms, moving us closer to a world where immersive digital experiences are an everyday reality.

The path ahead for Orion is filled with promise. As the glasses evolve, they have the potential to become more than just a niche product for early adopters—they could redefine how we interact with the digital world, much like the smartphone did a decade ago. With each iteration, Meta is building towards a future where AR glasses aren't just a luxury but a common part of life, bridging the gap between the digital and physical worlds in ways we're only beginning to explore.

Chapter Eight

Meta's Vision for the AR Landscape

Meta's vision for augmented reality goes far beyond just the Orion AR glasses. The company sees AR as part of a broader convergence of emerging technologies, where artificial intelligence, virtual reality, and augmented reality all merge to create a seamless digital ecosystem. AR will not operate in isolation; instead, it will work in tandem with AI to create more intuitive and responsive environments, while VR adds layers of immersive experience. For instance, AR could overlay the real world with digital information, while AI processes that data in real time, tailoring experiences to individual users. As these technologies continue to mature, the boundaries between them will blur, giving rise to new ways of interacting with the digital world that are both immersive and deeply integrated into everyday life.

Meta's long-term goals for augmented reality stretch beyond personal entertainment or professional use. The company envisions AR as a tool that could have a profound societal impact. Imagine classrooms where students can explore historical sites or complex scientific models in three dimensions, all from the comfort of their desks. AR could revolutionize education by making learning more interactive and engaging. In healthcare, surgeons might use AR to visualize patient anatomy during operations, enhancing precision and reducing risks. Meanwhile, in entertainment, augmented reality could take storytelling and gaming to unprecedented levels of immersion, allowing people to step into the worlds they've only seen on screens. The potential applications are vast, and Meta is positioning itself to be at the forefront of this AR-driven future.

Ultimately, the introduction of Orion represents the next major leap in augmented reality, one that could reshape how we interact with both the digital and physical worlds. The technology embedded in Orion hints at a future where our everyday experiences are enriched by digital layers that enhance productivity, creativity, and connection. By merging the power of AI, AR, and other emerging technologies, Meta is pushing towards a world where digital content is no longer confined to screens but is seamlessly woven into the fabric of our lives. This future will change not only how we work and play but how we communicate, learn, and interact with the world around us. Orion is just the beginning, but its potential signals a shift that could be as significant as the smartphone revolution—if not more.

Conclusion

As we look back on the development of Meta's Orion AR glasses, it's clear that they represent a significant milestone not only for augmented reality but for personal technology as a whole. The journey from initial concept to a working prototype has been one of immense innovation, overcoming challenges that once seemed insurmountable. Meta's vision of creating a device that could replace the smartphone has pushed the boundaries of what's possible, leading to the invention of groundbreaking technologies like microLED displays, silicon carbide waveguides, and neural interfaces. Each of these advancements is a testament to how far AR has come, yet it's only the beginning.

Looking forward, the future of AR is filled with potential. The Orion glasses are just one step towards a world where augmented reality becomes an integral part of our daily lives. As the technology continues to evolve, we can expect AR to move beyond niche applications and into the mainstream. Whether it's enhancing communication, transforming industries, or enriching our social interactions, AR will play a central role in how we experience the world. Meta is clearly positioning itself as a leader in this space, and their innovations will undoubtedly shape the future of AR and personal computing.

As we close, one thing is certain: the future of augmented reality is bright, and it's coming faster than we might expect. Stay curious, and follow this evolving landscape closely, because AR is poised to become as essential to daily life as the smartphone is today. With each new development, we'll see technologies like Orion take us one step closer to a reality where the digital and physical worlds coexist seamlessly, opening up possibilities we can only begin to imagine.

www.ingramcontent.com/pod-product-compliance
Lightning Source LLC
Chambersburg PA
CBHW070956220526
45471CB00007B/3048